Joseph Jastrow

THE MODERN OCCULT

For general information on our products and services, please contact us on prodinnova@mail.com

Printed in United States.

ISBN : 978-1532980367

10 9 8 7 6 5 4 3 2 1

Joseph Jastrow

THE MODERN OCCULT

Contents

The Modern Occult

IF that imaginary individual so convenient for literary illustration, a visitor from Mars, were to alight upon our planet at the present time, and if his intellectual interests induced him to take a survey of mundane views of what is "in heaven above, or on the earth beneath or in the waters under the earth," of terrestrial opinions in regard to the great problems of mind and matter, of government and society, of life and death—our Martian observer might conceivably report that a limited portion of mankind were guided by views that were the outcome of accumulated toil, and generations of studious devotion, representing a slow and tortuous, but progressive growth through error and superstition, and at the cost of persecution and bloodshed; that they maintained institutions of learning where the fruits of such thought could be imparted and the seeds cultivated to bear still more richly, but that outside of this respectable yet influential minority there were endless upholders of utterly unlike notions and of widely diverging beliefs, clamoring like the builders of the tower of Babel in diverse tongues.

It is well at least occasionally to remember that our conceptions of science and of truth, of the nature of logic and of evidence, are not so universally held as we unreflectingly assume or as we hopefully wish. Almost every one of the fundamental and indisputable tenets of science is regarded as hopelessly in error by some ardent would-be reformer. One Hampden declares that the earth is a motionless plane with the North Pole as the center; one Carpenter gives a hundred remarkable reasons why the earth is not round, with a challenge to the scientists of America to disprove them; one Symmes regarded the earth as hollow and habitable within, with openings at the poles which he offered to explore for the consideration of the "patronage of this and the new worlds"; while Symmes, Jr., explains how the interior is lighted, and that it probably forms the home of the lost tribes of Israel; and one Teed announces on equally conclusive evidence that the earth is a "stationary concave cell ... with people, Sun, Moon, Planets and Stars on the inside," the whole constituting an "alchemico-organic structure, a Gigantic Electro-Magnetic Battery." If we were to pass from opinions regarding the shape of the earth to the many other

Joseph Jastrow

and complex problems that appeal to human interests, it would be equally easy to collect 'ideas' comparable to these in value, evidence and eccentricity. With the conspicuously pathological outgrowth of brain-functioning —although its representatives in the literature of my topic are neither few nor far between— I shall not specifically deal; and yet the general abuse of logic, the helpless flounderings in the mire of delusive analogy, the baseless assumptions, which characterize insane or 'crank' productions, are readily found in modern occult literature.

The occult consists of a mixed aggregate of movements and doctrines, which may be the expressions of kindred interests and dispositions but present no essential community of content. Such members of this cluster of beliefs as in our day and generation have attained a considerable adherence or still retain it from former generations constitute the modern occult. The prominent characteristic of the occult is its marked divergence in trend and belief from the recognized standards and achievements of human thought. This divergence is one of attitude and logic and general perspective. It is a divergence of intellectual temperament that distorts the normal reactions to science and evidence and to the general significance and values of the factors of our complicated natures and our equally complicated environment. At least it is this in extreme and pronounced forms; and shades from it through an irregular variety of tints to a vague and often unconscious susceptibility for the unusual and eccentric, combined with an instability of conviction regarding established beliefs that is more often the expression of the weakness of ignorance than of the courage of independence. Occult doctrines are also likely to involve and to proceed upon mysticism and superstition; and their theme centers about such problems as the nature of mental action, the conception of life and death, the effect of cosmic conditions upon human events and endowment, the delineation of character, the nature and treatment of disease, or indeed about any of the larger or smaller realms of knowledge that combine with a strong human and possibly a practical interest, a considerable complexity of basal principles and general relations.

In surveying the more notable instances of the modern occult, it is well while bearing in mind the particular form of occultism or mysticism, or it may be merely of superstition and error, which one or another of the occult movements exhibits, to emphasize the importance of the intellectual motive or temperament that inclines to the occult. It is important to inquire not only what is believed, but what is the nature of the evidence that induces belief, what attracts and then makes converts, what the influences by which the belief spreads. Two classes of motives or interests are conspicuous; the one prominently intellectual or theoretical, the other moderately or grossly practical. Movements in which the former interest dominates contain elements that command respect even when they do not engage sympathy; they frequently appeal, though it may be unwisely, to worthy impulses and lofty aspirations. Amongst the movements presenting prominent practical aspects are to be found instances of the most irreverent and pernicious, as well as of the most vulgar, ignorant and fraudulent schemes which have been devised to mislead the human mind. Most occult movements, however, are of a mixed character, and in their career the speculative and the practical change in importance at different times or in different lands, or at the hands of variously minded leaders. Few escape and some seem especially designed for the partisanship of that class who are seeking whom they may devour; and stimulated by the greed for gain or the love for notoriety, set their snares for the eternally gullible. Fortunately, it must be added that the interest in the occult is under the sway of the law of fashion, and many a mental garment which is donned in spite of the protest of reason and propriety, is quietly laid aside when the dictum of the hour pronounces it unbecoming.

Historically considered, the occult points back to distant epochs and foreign civilizations; to ages when the facts of nature were but weakly grasped, when belief was largely dominated by the authority of tradition, when even the ablest minds fostered or assented to superstition, when the social conditions of life were inimical to independent thought and the mass of men were cut off from intellectual growth of even the most elementary kind. Pseudo-science flourished in the absence of true knowledge, and imaginative insight and unfounded belief held the office intended for inductive reason. Ignorance inevitably led to error and false views to false practices. In a sympathetic environment of this kind

Joseph Jastrow

the occultist flourished and displayed the impressive insignia of exclusive wisdom. His attitude was that of one seeking to solve an enigma, to find the key to a strange puzzle; his search was for some mystic charm, some talismanic formula, some magical procedure, which shall dispel the mist that hides the face of nature and expose her secrets to his ecstatic gaze. By one all-encompassing, masterful effort the correct solution was to be discovered or revealed; and at once and for all, ignorance would give place to true knowledge, science and nature become as an open book, doubt and despair be replaced by the serenity of perfect wisdom. As our ordinary senses and faculties are obviously insufficient to accomplish such ends, supernatural powers must be appealed to, a transcendental sphere of spiritual activity must be cultivated capable of perceiving through the hidden symbolism of apparent phenomena, the underlying relations of cosmic structure and final purposes. Long periods of training and devotion, seclusion from the world, contemplation of inner mysteries, lead the initiate through the various stages of adeptship up to the final plane of communion with the infinite and the comprehension of truth in all things. This form of occultism reaches its fullest and purest expression in Oriental wisdom-religions. These vie in interest to the historian with the mythology and philosophy of Greece and Rome; and we of the Occident feel free to profit by their ethical and philosophical content, and to cherish the impulses which gave them life. But when such views are forcibly transplanted to our age and clime, when they are decked in garments so unlike their original vestments, particularly when they are associated with dubious practices and come into violent conflict with the truth that has accumulated since they first had birth, their aspect is profoundly altered and they come within the circle of the modern occult.

Of this character is Theosophy, an occult movement brought into recent prominence by the works and personality of Mme. Blavatsky. The story of the checkered career of that remarkable woman is fairly accessible. Born in Russia in 1831 as Helen Petrovna, daughter of Colonel Hahn, of the Russian army, she was married at the age of seventeen to an elderly gentleman, M. Blavatsky. She is described in girlhood as a person of passionate temper and willful and erratic disposition. She separated or escaped from her husband after a few months of married life and entered upon an extended period of travel and adventure, in which 'psychic' experiences and the search for unusual persons and beliefs were prominent. She absorbed Hindu wisdom from the adepts of India; she sat at the feet of a thaumaturgist at Cairo; she journeyed to Canada to meet the medicine man of the Red Indians, and to New Orleans to observe the practices of Voodoo among the negroes. It is difficult to know what to believe in the accounts prepared by her enthusiastic followers. Violations of physical laws were constantly occurring in her presence, and "sporadic outbreaks of rappings and feats of impulsive pots, pans, beds and chairs insisted on making themselves notorious." In 1873 she came to New York and sat in 'spiritualistic' circles, assuming an assent to their theories, but claiming to see through and beyond the manifestations the operations of her theosophic guides in astral projection. At one of these séances she met Colonel Olcott and assisted him in the foundation of the Theosophical Society in New York in October, 1875. Mme. Blavatsky directed the thought of this society to the doctrines of Indian occultism, and reported the appearance in New York of a Hindu Mahatma, who left a turban behind him as evidence of his astral visit. Later Mme. Blavatsky and Colonel Olcott (who remained her staunch supporter, but whom she referred to in private as a 'psychologized baby') went to India and at Adyar established a shrine from which were mysteriously issued answers to letters placed within its recesses, from which inaccessible facts were revealed and a variety of interesting marvels performed. Discords arose within her household and led to the publication by M. and Mme. Coulomb, her confederates, of letters illuminating the tricks of the trade by which the miracles had been produced. Mme. Blavatsky pronounced the letters to be forgeries, but they were sufficiently momentous to bring Mr. Hodgson to India to investigate for the Society for Psychical Research. He was able to deprive many of the miracles of their mystery, to show how the 'shrine' from which the Mahatma's messages emanated was accessible to Mme. Blavatsky by the aid of sliding panels and secret drawers, to show that these messages were in style, spelling and handwriting the counterpart of Mme. Blavatsky's, to show that many of the phenomena were the result of planned collusion

Joseph Jastrow

and that others were created by the limitless credulity and the imaginative exaggeration of the witnesses — 'domestic imbeciles,' as madame confidentially called them. The report of the society convicted 'the Priestess of Isis' of "a long continued combination with other persons to produce by ordinary means a series of apparent marvels for the support of the Theosophic movement"; and concludes with these words: "For our own part, we regard her neither as the mouthpiece of hidden seers nor as a mere vulgar adventuress; we think that she has achieved a title to permanent remembrance as one of the most accomplished, ingenious and interesting impostors in history." Mme. Blavatsky died in 1891, and her ashes were divided between Adyar, London and New York.

The Theosophic movement continues, though with abated vigor, owing partly to the above-mentioned disclosures, but probably more to the increasing propagandism of other cults, to the lack of a leader of Mme. Blavatsky's genius, or to the inevitable ebb and flow of such interests. Mme. Blavatsky continued to expound Theosophy after the exposures, and Mrs. Besant, Mr. Sinnett and others were ready to take up the work at her death. However, miracles are no longer performed, and no immediately practical ends are proclaimed. Individual development and evolution, mystic discourses on adeptship and Karma and Maya and Nirvana, communion with the higher ends of life, the cultivation of an esoteric psychic insight, form the goal of present endeavor. The Mahatmas are giving "intellectual instructions, enormously more interesting than even the exhibition of their abnormal powers."… The modern Theosophist seeks to appeal to men and women of philosophical inclinations, for whom an element of mysticism has its charm, and who are intellectually at unrest with the conceptions underlying modern science and modern life. Such persons are quite likely to be well-educated, refined and sincere. We may believe them intellectually misguided; we may recognize the fraud to which their leader resorted to glorify her creed, but we must equally recognize the absence of many pernicious tendencies in their teachings which characterize other and more practical occult movements.

Spiritualism, another member of the modern occult family, presents a combination of features rather difficult to portray; but its public career of half a century has probably rendered its tenets and practices fairly familiar. For, like other movements, it presents both doctrines and manifestations, and, like other movements, it achieved its popularity through its manifestations and emphasized the doctrines to maintain the interest and solidarity of its numerous converts. Deliberate fraud has been repeatedly demonstrated in a large number of alleged 'spiritualistic' manifestations; in many more the very nature of the phenomena and of the conditions under which they appear is so strongly suggestive of trickery as to render any other hypothesis of their origin improbable and unnecessary. Unconscious deception, exaggerated and distorted reports, defective and misleading observation have been demonstrated to be most potent reagents, whereby alleged miracles are made to throw off their mystifying envelopings and to leave a simple deposit of intelligible and often commonplace fact. That the methods of this or that medium have not been brought within the range of such explanation may be admitted, but the admission carries with it no bias in favor of the spiritualistic hypothesis. It may be urged, however, that where there is much smoke there is apt to be some fire; yet there is little prospect of discovering the nature of the fire until the smoke has been completely cleared away. Perhaps it has been snatched from heaven by a materialized Prometheus; perhaps it may prove to be the trick of a ridiculus mus gnawing at a match. However, the main point to be insisted upon with regard to such manifestations is that their interpretation and their explanation demand technical knowledge and training, or at least special adaptability to such pursuits. "The problem cannot be solved and settled by amateurs, nor by 'common sense' that

Delivers brawling judgments all day long,

On all things unashamed."

Spiritualism represents a systematization of popular beliefs and superstitions, modified by echoes of religious and philosophical doctrines; and is thus not wholly occult. Its main purpose was to establish the reality of communication with departed spirits; the means which at first spontaneously presented themselves and later were devised for this purpose were in large measure not original. The rappings are in accord with the traditional folkore behavior of ghosts, though their transformation into a signal code may have been due to the originality of the Fox children; the planchette has its analogies in Chinese and European modes of divination; clairvoyance was incorporated from the phenomena of artificial somnambulism, as practiced by the successors of Mesmer; the 'sensitive' or 'medium' suggests the same origin as well as the popular belief in the gift of supernatural powers to favored individuals; others of the phenomena such as 'levitation' and 'cabinet performances' have counterparts in Oriental magic; 'slate-writing,' 'form materializations,' 'spirit-messages,' and 'spirit photographs' are, in the main, modern contributions. These various phenomena as ordinarily presented breed the typical atmosphere of the séance chamber, which resists precise analysis, but in which it is easy to detect morbid credulity, blind prepossession and emotional contagion; while the dependence of the phenomena on the character of the medium offers strong temptation alike to shrewdness, eccentricity and dishonesty. On the side of his teachings the spiritualist is likewise not strikingly original. The relations of his beliefs to those that grew about the revelations of Sweden- borg, to the speculations of the German 'pneumatologists' and to other philosophical doctrines, though perhaps not intimate, are yet traceable and interesting; and in another view the 'spiritualist' is as old as man himself and finds his antecedents in the necromancer of Chaldea, or in the Shaman of Siberia, or the Angekok of Greenland, or the spirit doctor of the Karens. The modern mediums are simply repeating with new costumes and improved scenic effects the mystic drama of primitive man.

Spiritualism thus appeals to a deep-seated craving in human nature, that of assurance of personal immortality and of communion with the departed. Just so long as a portion of mankind will accept material evidence of such a belief, and will even countenance the irreverence, the triviality and the vulgarity surrounding the manifestations, just so long as these persons will misjudge their own powers of detecting how the alleged supernatural appearances were really produced and remain unimpressed by the principles upon which alone a consistent explanation is possible, just so long will spiritualism and kindred delusions flourish.

As to the present day status of this cult it is not easy to speak positively. Its clientele has apparently greatly diminished; it still numbers amongst its adherents men and women of culture and education and many more who cannot be said to possess these qualities. There seems to be a considerable class of persons who believe that natural laws are insufficient to account for their personal experiences and those of others, and who temporarily or permanently incline to a spiritualistic hypothesis in preference to any other. Spiritualists of this intellectual temper can, however, form but a small portion of those who are enrolled under its creed. If one may judge by the tone and contents of current spiritualistic literature, the rank and file to which Spiritualism appeals present an unintellectual occult company, credulously accepting what they wish to believe, utterly regardless of the intrinsic significance of evidence or hypothesis, vibrating from one extreme or absurdity to another, and blindly following a blinder or more fanatic leader or a self-interested charlatan. While for the most extravagant and unreasonable expressions of Spiritualism one would probably turn to the literature of a few decades ago, yet the symptoms presented by the Spiritualism of today are unmistakably of the same character, and form a complex as characteristic as the symptom-complex of hysteria or epilepsy, and which, faute de mieux, may be termed occult. It is a type of occultism of a particularly pernicious character because of its power to lead a parasitic life upon the established growths of religious beliefs and interests, and at the same time to administer to the needs of an unfortunate but widely prevalent passion for special signs and omens and the interpretation of personal experiences. It is a weak though comprehensible nature that becomes bewildered in the presence of a few experiences that seem homeless among the generous provisions of modern science, and runs off panic-stricken to find shelter in a system that satisfies a narrow personal craving at the sacrifice of broadly established principles, nurtured and grown strong in the hardy and beneficent atmosphere of science. It is a weaker and an ignorant nature that is attracted to the cruder forms of such beliefs, be it by the impulsive yielding to emotional susceptibility, by the contagion of an unfortunate mental environment, or by the absence of the steadying power of religious faith or of logical vigor or of confidence in the knowledge of others. Spiritualism finds converts

Joseph Jastrow

in both camps and assembles them under the flag of the occult.[1]

The wane in the popularity of Spiritualism may be due in part to frequent exposures, in part to the passing of the occult interest to pastures new, and in part to other and less accessible causes. Such interest may again become dominant by the success or innovations of some original medium or by the appearance of some unforeseen circumstances; at present there is a disposition to take up 'spiritual healing' and 'spiritual readings of the future' rather than mere assurances from the dead, and thus to emulate the practical success of more recently established rivals. The history of Spiritualism, by its importance and its extravagance of doctrine and practice, forms an essential and an instructive chapter in the history of belief; and

---

1 To prevent misunderstanding it is well to repeat that I am speaking of the general average of thorough-going spiritualists. The fact that a few mediums have engaged the attention of scientifically minded investigators has no bearing on the motives which lead most persons to make a professional call on a medium, or to join a circle. The further fact that these investigators have at times found themselves baffled by the medium's performances, and that a few of them have announced their readiness to accept the spiritualistic hypothesis is of importance in some aspects, but does not determine the general trend of the spiritualistic movement in the direction in which it Is considered in the present discussion. It may also prevent misunderstanding of other parts of my presentation to continue this footnote by adding that I desire to distinguish sharply between the occult and what has unwisely been termed Psychical Research — unwisely because such research is either truly psychological and requires no differentiation from other allied and legitimate research, or it is something other than psychological which is inaptly expressed by calling it 'psychical.' I admit and emphasize that the majority of such research is the result of a scientific motive and is far removed from the occult. I therefore shall say nothing of Psychical Research and regret that it is necessary even to deny its possible inclusion in the occult. Such inclusion is. however, suggested by much that is talked of and written under the name of Psychic Research, and there can be no doubt that the interest of many members of Psychic Research Societies and of readers of their publications, is essentially of an occult nature. Whatever in these publications seems to favor mystery and to substantiate supernormal powers is readily absorbed, and its bearings fancifully interpreted and exaggerated; the more critical and successfully explanatory papers meet with a less extended and less sensational reception. Unless most wisely directed, Psychic Research is likely, by not letting the right hand know what the left hand is doing, to foster the undesirable propensities of human nature as rapidly as it antagonizes them. Like indiscriminate aims-giving it has the possibilities of affording relief and of making paupers at the same time. While I regard the acceptance of telepathy as an established phenomenon, as absolutely unwarranted and most unfortunate, and while I feel a keen personal regret that men whose ability and opinions I estimate highly have announced their belief in a spiritualistic explanation of their personal experiences with a particular medium, yet my personal regret and my logical disapproval of these conclusions have obviously no bearing upon the general questions under discussion. The scientific investigation of the same phenomena which have formed the subject matter of occult beliefs, is radically different in motive, method and result from the truly occult.

The Modern Occult

there is no difficulty in tracing the imprints of its footsteps on the sands of the occult.

The impress of ancient and mediaeval lore upon latter-day occultism is conspicuous in the survivals of Alchemy and Astrology. Phrenology represents a more recent pseudo-science, but one sufficiently obsolete to be considered under the same head, as may also Palmistry, which has relations both to an ancient form of divination and to a more modern development after the manner of Physiognomy. The common characteristic of these is their devotion to a practical end. Alchemy occupies a somewhat distinct position. The original alchemists sought the secret of converting the baser metals into gold, in itself a sufficiently alluring and human occupation. There is no reason why such a problem should assume an occult aspect, except the sufficient one that ordinary procedures have not proved capable to effect the desired end. It is a proverbial fault of ambitious inexperience to attack valiantly large problems with endless confidence and sweeping aspiration. It is well enough in shaping your ideas to hitch your wagon to a star; yet the temporary utility of horses need not be overlooked; but shooting arrows at the stars is apt to prove an idle pastime. If we are willing to forget for the moment that the same development of logic and experiment that makes possible the mental and material equipment of the modern chemist makes impossible his consideration of the alchemist's search, we may note how far the inherent constitution of the elements, to say nothing of their possible transmutation, has eluded his most ultimate analysis. How immeasurably farther it was removed from the grasp of the alchemist can hardly be expressed. But this is a scientific and not an occult view of the matter; it was not by progressive training in marksmanship that the occultist hoped to send his arrows to the stars. His was a mystic search for the magical transmutation, the elixir of life or the philosopher's stone. One might suppose that once the world has agreed that these ends are past finding out, the alchemist, like the maker of stone arrow-heads, would have found his occupation gone and have left no successor. His modern representative, however, is an interesting and by no means extinct species. He seems to flourish in France, but may be found in Germany, in England and in this country. He is rarely a pure

Joseph Jastrow

alchemist (although so recently as 1854 one of them offered to manufacture gold for the French mint), but represents the pure type of occultist. He calls himself a Rosicrucian; he establishes a university of the higher studies and becomes a Professor of Hermetic Philosophy. His thought is mystic, and symbolism has an endless fascination for him. The mystic significance of numbers, extravagant analogies of correspondence, the traditional hidden meanings of the Kabbalah fairly intoxicate him; and verbose accounts of momentous relations and of unintelligible discoveries run riot in his writings. His science is not a mere Chemistry, but a Hyper-Chemistry; his transmutations are not merely material but spiritual. Like all followers of an esoteric belief, he must stand apart from his fellow-men; he must cultivate the higher 'psychic' powers so that eventually he may be able by the mere action of his will to cause the atoms to group themselves into gold.

The modern alchemist is, however, a general occultist; he may be also an astrologer or a magnetist or a theosophist. But he is foremost an ardent enthusiast for exclusive and unusual lore—not the common and superficial possessions of misguided democratic science. He goes through the forms of study, remains superior to the baser practical ends of life, and finds his reward in the self-satisfaction of exclusive wisdom. In Paris, at least, he forms part of a rather respectable salon, speaking socially, or a 'company of educated charlatans,' speaking scientifically. His class does not constitute a large proportion of modern occultists, but they present a prominent form of its intellectual temperament. "There are also people," says Mr. Lang, "who so dislike our detention in the prison house of old unvarying laws that their bias is in favor of anything which may tend to prove that science in her contemporary mood is not infallible. As the Frenchman did not care what sort of a scheme he invested money in, provided that it annoys the English, so many persons do not care what they invest belief in, provided that it irritates men of science." Of such is the kingdom of alchemists and their brethren.

Astrology, phrenology, physiognomy and palmistry have in common a search for knowledge whereby to regulate the affairs of life, to foretell the future, to comprehend one's destiny and capabilities. They aim to secure success or at least to be forearmed against failure by being forewarned. This is a natural, a practical, and in no essential way, an occult desire. It becomes occult, or better, superstitious, when it is satisfied by appeals to relations and influences which do not exist, and by false interpretation of what may be admitted as measurably and vaguely true and about equally important. When not engaged in their usual occupation of building most startling superstructures on the weakest foundations, practical occultists are like Dr. Holmes' katydid, "saying an undisputed thing in such a solemn way." They will not hearken to the experience of the ages that success cannot be secured nor character read by discovering their mystic stigmata; they will not learn from physiology and psychology that the mental capabilities, the moral and emotional endowment of an individual are not stamped on his body so that they may be revealed by half an hour's use of the calipers and tape-measure; they will not listen when science and common sense unite in teaching that the knowledge of mental powers is not such as may be applied by rule of thumb to individual cases, but that like much other valuable knowledge, it proceeds by the exercise of sound judgment, and must as a rule rest content with suggestive generalizations and imperfectly established correlations. An educated man with wholesome interests and a vigorous logical sense can consider a possible science of character and the means of aiding its advance without danger and with some profit. But this meat is sheer poison to those who are usually attracted to such speculations, while it offers to the unscrupulous charlatan a most convenient net to spread for the unwary. In so far as these occult mariners, the astrologists and phrenologists and id genus omne are sincere, and in so far represent superstition rather than commercial fraud, they simply ignore through obstinacy or ignorance the light -houses and charts and the other aids to modern navigation, and persist in steering their craft by an occult compass. In some cases they are professedly setting out, not for any harbor marked on terrestrial maps, but their expedition is for the golden fleece or for the apples of the Hesperides; and with loud-voiced advertisements of their skill as pilots, they proceed to form stock companies for the promotion of the enterprise and to sell the shares to credulous speculators.

It would be a profitless task to review the alleged data of astrology

Joseph Jastrow

or phrenology or palmistry except for the illustrations which they readily yield of the nature of the conceptions and the logic which command a certain popular interest and acceptance. The interest in these notions, is, as Mr. Lang argues about ghosts and rappings and bogles, in how they come to be believed rather than in how much or how little they chance to be true. In examining the professed evidence for the facts and laws and principles (sit venia verbis) that pervade astrology or phrenology or palmistry or dream-interpretation, or beliefs of that ilk, we find the flimsiest kind of texture that will hardly bear examination and holds together only so long as it is kept secluded from the light of day. Far-fetched analogy, baseless assertion, the uncritical assimilation of popular superstitions, a great deal of prophecy after the event —it is wonderful how clearly the astrologer finds the indications of Napoleon's career in his horoscope, or the phrenologist reads them in the Napoleonic cranial protuberances—much fanciful elaboration of de- tail, ringing the variations on a sufficiently complex and non-demonstrable proposition, cultivating a convenient vagueness of expression together with an apologetic skill in providing for and explaining exceptions, the courage to ignore failure and the shrewdness to profit by coincidences and half-assimilated smatterings of science; and with it all an insensibility to the moral and intellectual demands of the logical decalogue, and you have the skeleton which clothed with one flesh be- comes astrology, and with another phrenology and with another palmistry or solar biology or descriptive mentality or what not. Such pseudo- sciences thrive upon that widespread and intense craving for practical guidance of our individual affairs, which is not satisfied with judicious applications of general principles, with due consideration of the probabilities and uncertainties of human life, but demands an impossible and precise revelation. Not all that passes for, and in a way is, knowledge, is or is likely soon to become scientific; and when a peasant parades in an academic gown the result is likely to be a caricature.

To achieve fortune, to judge well and command one's fellow-men, to foretell and control the future, to be wise in worldly lore, are natural objects of human desire; but still another is essential to happiness. Whether we attempt to procure these good fortunes by going early to bed and early to rise, or by more occult procedures, we wish to be healthy as well as wealthy and wise. The maintenance of health and the perpetuity of youth were not absent from the mediaeval occultist's search, and formed an essential part of the benefits to be conferred by the elixir of life and the philosopher's stone. A series of superstitions and extravagant systems are conspicuous in the antecedents and the bye- paths of the history of medicine, and are related to it much as astrology is to astronomy or alchemy to chemistry; and because medicine in part remains, and to previous generations was conspicuously an empirical art rather than a science, it offers great opportunity for practical error and misapplied partial knowledge. It is not necessary to go back to early civilizations or to primitive peoples, among whom the medicine- man and the priest were one and alike appealing to occult powers, nor to early theories of disease which beheld in insanity the obsession of demons and resorted to exorcism to cast them out; it is not necessary to consider the various personages who acquired notoriety as healers by laying on of hands or by appeal to faith, or who like Mesmer introduced the system of Animal Magnetism, or like some of his followers, sought directions for healing from the clairvoyant dicta of somnambules; it is not necessary to ransack folk-lore superstitions and popular remedies for the treatment of disease; for the modern forms of 'irregular 1 healing offer sufficient illustrations of occult methods of escaping the ills that flesh is heir to.

The existence of a special term for a medical impostor is doubtless the result of the prevalence of the class thus named, but quackery and occult medicine though mutually overlapping, can by no means be held accountable for one another's failings. Many forms of quackery proceed on the basis of superstitions or fanciful or exaggerated notions containing occult elements, but for the present purpose it is wise to limit attention to those in which this occult factor is distinctive; for medical quackery in its larger relations is neither modern nor occult. Occult healing takes its distinctive character from the theory underlying the practice rather than from the nature of the practice. It is not so much what is done as why it is done or pretended to be done or not done, that determines its occult character. A factor of prominence in modern

Joseph Jastrow

occult healing is indeed one that in other forms characterized many of its predecessors and was rarely wholly absent from the connection between the procedure and the result; this is the mental factor, which may be called upon to give character to a theory of disease, or be utilized consciously or unconsciously as a curative principle. It is not implied that 'mental medicine' is necessarily and intrinsically occult, but only that the general trend of modern occult notions regarding disease may be best portrayed in certain typical forms of 'psychic' healing. The legitimate recognition of the importance of mental conditions in health and disease is one of the results of the union of modern psychology and modern medicine. An exaggerated and extravagant as well as pretentious and illogical over-statement and misstatement of this principle may properly be considered as occult.

Among such systems there is one which by its momentary prominence overshadows all others, and for this reason as well as for its more explicit or rather extended statement of principles, must be accorded special attention. I need hardly say that I refer to that egregious misnomer, Christian Science. This system is said to have been discovered by or revealed to Mrs. Mary Baker Glover Eddy in 1860. Several of its most distinctive positions (without their religious setting) are to be found in the writings and were used in the practice of Mr. or Dr. P. P. Quimby (1802-1866), whom Mrs. Eddy professionally consulted shortly before she began her own propagandum. On its theoretical side the system presents a series of quasi-metaphysical principles, and also a professed interpretation of the Scriptures; on its practical side it offers a means of curing or avoiding disease and includes under disease also what is more generally described as sin and misfortune. With Christian Science as a religious movement I shall not directly deal; I wish, however, to point out that this assumption of a religious aspect finds a parallel in Spiritualism and Theosophy and doubtless forms one of the most potent reasons for the success of these occult movements. It would be a most dangerous principle to admit that the treatment of disease and the right to ignore hygiene can become the perquisite of any religious faith. It would be equally unwarranted to permit the principles which are responsible for such beliefs to take shelter behind the ramparts of religious tolerance;

for the essential principles of Christian Science do not constitute a form of Christianity any more than they constitute a science; but in so far as they do not altogether elude description, pertain to the domain over which medicine, physiology and psychology hold sway. As David Harum, in speaking of his church-going habits, characteristically explains, "the one I stay away from when I don't go's the Prespyteriun," so the doctrines which Christian Science 'stays away from' are those over which recognized departments of academic learning have the authority to decide.

Mrs. Eddy's magnum opus serving at once as the text-book of the 'science' and as a revised version of the Scriptures —Science and Health, with Key to the Scriptures— has been circulated to the extent of one hundred and seventy thousand copies. I shall not give an account of this book nor subject its more tangible tenets to a logical review; I must be content to recommend its pages as suggestive reading for the student of the occult and to set forth in the credentials of quotation marks some of the dicta concerning disease. Yet it may be due to the author of this system to begin by citing what are declared to be its fundamental tenets, even if their connection with what is built upon them is far from evident.

"The fundamental propositions of Christian Science are summarized in the four following, to me self-evident propositions. Even if read backward, these propositions will be found to agree in statement and proof:

1. God is All in all.

2. God is good. Good is Mind.

3. God, Spirit, being all, nothing is matter. 4. Life, God, omnipotent Good, deny death, evil, sin, disease—Dis- ease, sin, evil, death, deny Good, omnipotent God, Life."

"What is termed disease does not exist." "Matter has no being." "All is mind." "Matter is but the subjective state of what is here termed mortal mind." "All disease is the result of education, and can carry its ill-effects no farther than mortal mind maps out the way." "The fear of dissevered bodily members, or a belief in such a possibility, is reflected on the body, in the shape of headache, fractured bones, dis- located joints, and so on, as directly as shame is seen rising to the cheek. This human error about physical

Joseph Jastrow

wounds and colics is part and parcel of the delusion that matter can feel and see, having sensation and substance." "Insanity implies belief in a diseased brain, while physical ailments (so-called) arise from belief that some other portions of the body are deranged. ... A bunion would produce insanity as perceptible as that produced by congestion of the brain, were it not that mortal mind calls the bunion an unconscious portion of the body. Reverse this belief and the results would be different." "We weep because others weep, we yawn because they yawn, and we have small-pox because others have it; but mortal mind, not matter, contains and carries the infection." "A Christian Scientist never gives medicine, never recommends hygiene, never manipulates." "Anatomy, Physiology, Treatises on Health, sustained by what is termed material law, are the husbandmen of sickness and disease." "You can even educate a healthy horse so far in physiology that he will take cold without his blanket." "If exposure to a draught of air while in a state of perspiration is followed by chills, dry cough, influenza, congestive symptoms in the lungs, or hints of inflammatory rheumatism, your Mind-remedy is safe and sure. If you are a Christian Scientist, such symptoms will not follow from the exposure; but if you believe in laws of matter and their fatal effects when transgressed, you are not fit to conduct your own case or to destroy the bad effects of belief. When the fear subsides and the conviction abides that you have broken no law, neither rheumatism, consumption nor any other disease will ever result from exposure to the weather." "Destroy fear and you end the fever." "To prevent disease or cure it mentally let spirit destroy the dream of sense. If you wish to heal by argument, find the type of the ailment, get its name and array your mental plea against the physical. Argue with the patient (mentally, not audibly) that he has no disease, and conform the argument to the evidence. Mentally insist that health is the everlasting fact, and sickness the temporal falsity. Then realize the presence of health and the corporeal senses will respond, so be it." "My publications alone heal more sickness than an unconscientious student can begin to reach." "The quotient when numbers have been divided by a fixed rule, are not more unquestionable than the scientific tests I have made of the effects of truth upon the sick." "I am never mistaken in my scientific diagnosis of disease." "Outside of

Christian Science all is vague and hypothetical, the opposite of Truth." "Outside Christian Science all is error."

Surely this is a remarkable product of mortal mind! It would perhaps be an interesting tour de force, though hardly so entertaining as 'Alice in Wonderland,' to construct a universe on the assertions and hypotheses which Christian Science presents; but it would have less resemblance to the world we know than has Alice's Wonderland. For any person for whom logic and evidence are something more real than ghosts or myths, the feat must always be relegated to the airy realm of the imagination and must not be brought in contact with earthly realities. And yet the extravagance of Mrs. Eddy's book, its superb disdain of vulgar fact, its transcendental self-confidence, its solemn assumption that reiteration and variation of assertion somehow spontaneously generate proof or self-evidence, its shrewd assimilation of a theological flavor, its occasional successes in producing a presentable travesty of scientific truth — all these distinctions may be found in many a dust-covered volume, that represents the intensity of conviction of some equally enthusiastic and equally inspired occultist, but one less successful in securing a chorus to echo his refrain.

I cannot dismiss 'Eddyism' without illustrating the peculiar structures under which, in an effort to be consistent, it is forced to take shelter. Since disease is always of purely mental origin, it follows that disease and its symptoms cannot ensue without the conscious cooperation of the patient; since "Christian Science divests material drugs of their imaginary power," it follows that the labels on the bottles that stand on the druggist's shelves are correspondingly meaningless. And it becomes an interesting problem to inquire how the consensus of mortal mind came about that associates one set of symptoms with prussic acid, and another with alcohol, and another with quinine. Inhaling oxygen or common air would prepare one for the surgeon's knife, and prussic acid or alcohol have no more effect than water, if only a congress of nations would pronounce the former to be anaesthetic and promulgate a decree that the latter shall be harmless. Christian Science does not flinch from this position. "If a dose of poison is swallowed through mistake and the patient dies, even though physician and patient are expecting favorable results, does belief, you ask, cause this death? Even so, and as directly as if the poison had been intentionally taken. In such cases a few persons believe the potion swallowed by the patient to be harmless; but the vast majority of mankind, though they know nothing of this particular case and this special person, believe the arsenic, the strychnine, or whatever the drug used, to be poisonous, for it has been set down as a poison by mortal mind. The consequence is that the result is controlled by the majority of opinions outside, not by the infinitesimal minority of opinions in the sick chamber." But why should the opinions of   οἱ πολλοὶ   be of influence in such a case, and the enlightened minorities be sufficient to effect the marvelous cures in all the other cases? Christian Scientists do not take cold in draughts in spite of the contrary opinions or illusions of misguided majorities. The logical Christian Scientist need not eat. "for the truth is food does not affect the life of man," and should not renounce his faith by adding, "but it would be foolish to venture beyond our present understanding foolish to stop eating, until we gain more goodness and a clearer comprehension of the living God." And if he is a mental physician he must be a mental surgeon, too, and not plead that, "Until the advancing age admits the efficacy and supremacy of mind, it is better to leave the adjustment of broken bones and dislocations to the fingers of surgeons." But it is unprofitable to consider the weakness of any occult system in its encounters with actual science and actual fact. It is simply as a real and prominent menace to rationality that these doctrines naturally attract consideration. As illustrations of present-day occult beliefs we are naturally tempted to inquire what measure of (perverted) truth they may contain; but the more worthy question is, How do such perversions come to find so large a company of 'supporting listeners'? For to anyone who can read and be convinced by the sequence of words of this system, ordinary logic has no power, and to him the world of reality brings no message. No form of the modern occult antagonizes the foundations of science so brusquely as this one. The possibility of science rests on the thorough and absolute distinction between the subjective and the objective. In what measure a man loses the power to draw this distinction clearly and as other men do, in that

The Modern Occult

measure he becomes irrational and insane. The objective exists; and no amount of thinking it away, or thinking it differently, will change it. That is what is understood by ultimate scientific truth; something that will endure unmodified by passing ways of viewing it, open to every one's verification who can come equipped with the proper means to verify — a permanent objective to be ascertained by careful logical inquiry, not to be determined by subjective opinion. Logic is the language of science; Christian Science and what sane men call science can never communicate because they do not speak the same language.

It would be unfortunate if in emphasizing the popular preeminence of Christian Science, one were to overlook the significance of the many other forms of 'drugless healing' which bid for public favor by appeal to ignorance and to occult and superstitious instincts. Some are allied to Christian Science and like it assimilate their cult to a religious movement; others are unmistakably the attempts of charlatans to lure the credulous by noisy advertisements of newly discovered and scientifically indorsed systems of 'psychic force,' or some personal 'ism.' For many purposes it would be unjust to group together such various systems, which in the nature of things must include sinner and saint, the misguided sincere, the half-believers who think 'there may be something in it,' or 'that it is worth a trial,' along with scheming quacks and adepts in commercial fraud. They illustrate the many and various roads traveled in the search for health by pilgrims who are dissatisfied with the highways over which medical science goes its steady, though it may be, uncertain gait. Among them there is both plausible exaggeration and ignorant perversion and dishonest libel of the relations that bind together body and mind. Among the several schisms from the Mother Church of Christian Science there is one that claims to be the 'rational phase of the mental healing doctrine/ that acknowledges the reality of disease and the incurability of serious organic disorders and resents any connection with the "half-fanatical personality worship [of Mrs. Eddy] as quite as foreign to its tenets as would be the views of the Tree Religious Association' to the Tope of Rome.' 'Divine Healing' exhibits its success in one notable instance, in the establishment of a school and college, a bank, a land and investment association, a

Joseph Jastrow

printing and publishing office and sundry Divine Healing Homes; and this prosperity is now to be extended by the foundation of a city or colony of converts who shall be united by the common bond of faith in divine healing as transmitted in the personal power of their leader. The official organ of this movement announces that the personification of their faith "makes her religion a business and conducts herself upon sound business principles." With emphatic protest on the part of each that he alone holds the key to salvation, and that his system is quite original and unlike any other, comes the procession of Metaphysical Healer and Mind-Curist and Viticulturist and Magnetic Healer and Astrological Health Guide and Phrenopathist and Medical Clairvoyant and Psychic Scientist and Mesmerist and Occultist. Some use or abuse the manipulations of Hypnotism; others claim the power to concentrate the magnetism of the air and to excite the vital fluids by arousing the proper mental vibrations, or by some equally lucid and demonstrable procedure; some advertise magnetic cups and positive and negative powders and absent treatment by outputs of 'psychic force' and countless other imposing devices. In truth, they form a motley crew, and with their 'Colleges of Fine Forces' and 'Psychic Research Companies,' offering diplomas and degrees for a three weeks' course of study or the reading of a book, represent the slums of the occult. An account of their methods is likely to be of as much interest to the student of fraud as to the student of opinion.

There can be no doubt that many of these systems have been stimulated into life or into renewed vigor by the success of 'Christian Science'; this is particularly noticeable in the introduction of absent treatment as a plank in their diverse platforms. This ingenious method of restoring the health of their patients and their own exchequers appealed to all the band of healing occultists from Spiritualist to Vibrationist, as easily adaptable to their several systems. In much the same way Mesmer, more than a hundred years ago, administered to the practice which had exhausted the capacity of his personal attention by magnetizing trees and selling magnetized water. The absent treatment represents the occult 'extension movement'; and unencumbered by the hampering restrictions of physical forces, superior even to wireless telegraphy, carries its influence into the remotest homes. From ocean to ocean and from North to South these absent healers set apart some hour of the day when they mentally convey their healing word to the scattered members of their flock. On the payment of a small fee you are made acquainted with the 'soul-communion time-table' for your longitude and may know when to meet the healing vibrations as they pass by. Others disdain any such temporal details and assure a cure merely on payment of the fee; the healer will know sympathetically when and how to transmit the curative impulses. Poverty and bad habits as well as disease readily succumb to the magic of the absent treatment. Here is the hysterical edict of one of them: 'Join the Success Circle'… "The Centre of that Circle is my omnipotent WORD. Daily I speak it. Its vibrations radiate more and more powerfully day by day. As the sun sends out vibrations … so my WORD radiates Success to 10,000 lives as easily as to one."

It is impossible to appreciate fully the extravagances of these occult healers unless one makes a sufficient sacrifice of time and patience to read over a considerable sample of the periodical publications with which American occultism is abundantly provided. And when one has accomplished this task he is still at sea to account for the readers and believers who support these various systems so undreamt of in our philosophy. It would really seem that there is no combination of ideas too absurd to fail entirely of a following. Carlyle without special provocation concluded that there were about forty million persons in England, mostly fools; what would have been his comment in the face of this vast array of human folly! If it be urged in rejoinder that beneath all this rubbish heap a true jewel lies buried, that the wonderful cures and the practical success of these various systems indicate their dependence upon an essential and valuable factor in the cure of disease and the formation of habits, it is possible with reservation to assent and with emphasis to demur. Such success, in so far as it is rightly reported, exemplifies the truly remarkable function of the mental factor in the control of normal as of disordered physiological functions. This truth has been recognized and utilized in unobtrusive ways for many generations, and within recent years has received substantial elaboration from carefully conducted experiments and observations. Specifically the therapeutic action of suggestion, both in its more usual forms

Joseph Jastrow

and as hypnotic suggestion, has shown to what unexpected extent such action may proceed in susceptible individuals. The well-informed and capable physician requires no instruction on this point; his medical education furnishes him with the means of determining the symptoms of true organic disorder, of functional derangement and of the modifications of these under the more or less unconscious interference of an unfortunate nervous system. It is quite as human for the physician as for other mortals to err, and there is doubtless as wide a range among them as among other pursuits, of ability, tact and insight. 'But when all is said and done' the fundamental fact remains that the utilization of the mental factor in the alleviation of disease will be best administered by those who are specifically trained in the knowledge of bodily and mental symptoms of disease. Such application of an established scientific principle may prove to be a jewel of worth in the hands of him who knows how to cut and set it. The difference between truth and error, between science and superstition, between what is beneficent to mankind and what is pernicious, frequently lies in the interpretation and the spirit as much as or more than in the fact. The utilization of mental influences in health and disease becomes the one or the other according to the wisdom and the truth and the insight into the real relations of things that guide its application. As far removed as chemistry from alchemy, as astronomy from astrology, as the doctrine of the localization of function in the brain from phrenology, as 'animal magnetism' from hypnotic suggestion, are the crude and perverse notions of Christian Scientist or Metaphysical Healer removed from the rational application of the influence of the mind over the body.

The growth and development of the occult forms an interesting problem in the psychology of belief. The motives that induce the will to believe in the several doctrines that have been passed in review are certainly not more easy to detect and to describe than would be the case in reference to the many other general problems—philosophical, scientific, religious, social, political or educational—on which the right to an opinion seems to be regarded as an inalienable heritage of humanity or at least of democracy. Professor James tells us that often "our faith is faith in someone else's faith, and in the greatest matters this is most the case." Certainly the waves of popularity of one cult and another reflect the potent influence of contagion in the formation of opinion and the direction of conduct. When we look upon the popular delusions of the past through the achromatic glasses which historical remoteness from present conditions enables us to adjust to our eyes, we marvel that humanity could have been so grossly misled, that obvious relations and fallacies could have been so stupidly overlooked, that worthless and prejudiced evidence could have been accepted as sound and significant. But the opinions to which we incline are all colored o'er with the deep tinge of emotional reality, which is the living expression of our interest in them or our inclination toward them. What they require is a more vigorous infusion of the pale cast of thought; for the problem of the occult and the temptations to belief which it holds out are such as can be met only by a vigorous and critical application of a scientific logic. As logical acumen predominates over superficial plausibility, as belief comes to be formed and evidence estimated according to its intrinsic value rather than according to its emotional acceptability, the propagandum of the occult will meet with greater resistance and aversion.

The fixation of belief proceeds under the influence of both general and special forces; the formation of a belief is at once a personal and a social reaction — a reaction to the evidence which recorded and personal experience presents and to the beliefs current in our environment, and this reaction is further modified by the temperament of the reagent. And although individual beliefs, however complex, are neither matters of chance nor are their causes altogether past finding out, yet some of their contributing factors are so vague and so inaccessible that they are most profitably considered as particular results of more or less clearly discerned general principles; and in many respects there is more valid interest in the general principles than in the particular results. It is interesting and it may be profitable to investigate why this area is wooded with oak and that with maple, but it is somewhat idle to speculate why this particular tree happens to be a maple rather than an oak, even if it chances to stand on our property, and to have an interest to us beyond all other trees. It is this false concentration of the attention to the personal and

Joseph Jastrow

individual result that is responsible for much unwarranted belief in the occult. It is likely that no single influence is more potent in this direction than this unfortunate over-interest in one's own personality and the consequent demand for a precise explanation of one's individual experiences. This habit seems to me a positive vice, and I am glad to find support in Professor James: "The chronic belief of mankind that events may happen for the sake of their personal significance is an abomination." Carried over to the field of subjective experiences, this habit sees in coincidences peculiarly significant omens and portents, not definitely and superstitiously, it may be, but sufficiently to obscure the consideration of the experience in any other than a personal light. The victim of this habit will remain logically unfit to survive the struggle against the occult. Only when the general problem is recognized as more significant for the guidance of belief than the attempted explicit personal explanations will these problems stand out in their true relations. It is interesting to note that the partaking of mince-pie at evening may induce bad dreams, but it is hardly profitable to speculate deeply why my dream took the form of a leering demon with the impolite habit of squatting on my chest. The stuff that dreams are made of is not susceptible of that type of analysis. The most generous allowance must be made for coincidences and irrelevancies, and it must be constantly remembered that the obscure phenomena of psychology, and, indeed, the phenomena of more thoroughly established and intrinsically more definite sciences, cannot be expected to pass the test of detailed and concrete combinations of circumstances. In other classes of knowledge the temptation to demand such explicit explanations of observations and experiences is not so strong because of the absence of an equally strong personal interest; but that clearly does not affect the logical status of the problem. The reply to this argument I can readily anticipate; and I confess that my admiration of Hamlet is somewhat dulled by reason of that ill-advised remark to Horatio about there being more things in heaven and earth than are dreamt of in our philosophies. The occultist always seizes upon that citation to refute the scientist. He prints it as his motto on his books and journals, and regards it as a slow poison that will in time effect the destruction of the rabble of scientists and reveal

The Modern Occult

the truth of his own Psycho-Harmonic Science or Heliocentric Astrology. It is one thing to be open-minded and to realize the incompleteness of scientific knowledge and to appreciate how often what was ignored by one generation has become the science of the next; and it is a very different thing to be impressed with coincidences and dreams and premonitions, and to regard them as giving the keynote to the conceptions of nature and reality, and to look upon science as a misdirected effort. Such differences of attitude depend frequently upon a difference of temperament as well as upon intellectual discernment; the man or the woman who flies to the things not dreamt of in our philosophy quite commonly does not understand the things which our philosophy very creditably accounts for. The two types of mind are different, and (I am again citing Professor James) "the scientific-academic mind and the feminine-mystical mind shy from each other's facts just as they fly from each other's temper and spirit."

Certain special influences combine with these fundamental differences of attitude to favor the spread of belief in the occult; and of these the character of the beliefs as of the believers furnish some evidence. At various stages of the discussion I have referred to the deceptive nature of the argument by analogy; to the dominating sympathy with a conclusion and the resulting assimilation and overestimation of apparent evidence in its favor; to the frequent failure to understand that the formation of valid opinion and the interpretation of evidence in any field of inquiry require somewhat of expert training and special aptitude, obviously so in technical matters, but only moderately less so in matters misleadingly regarded as general; to bias and superstition, to the weakness that bends easily to the influences of contagion, to unfortunate educational limitations and perversions and, not the least, to a defective grounding in the nature of scientific fact and proof. The mystery attaching to the behavior of the magnet led Mesmer to call his curative influence 'animal magnetism'—a conception that still prevails among latter-day occultists. The principle of sympathetic vibration, in obedience to which a tuning-fork takes up the vibrations of another in unison with it. is violently transferred to imaginary brain vibrations and to still more imaginary telepathic currents. The X-ray and wireless telegraphy

Joseph Jastrow

are certain to be utilized in corroboration of unproven modes of mental action, and will be regarded as the key to clairvoyance and rapport, just as well-known electrical phenomena have given rise to the notions of positive and negative temperaments and mediumistic polar attraction and repulsion. All this results from the absurd application of analogies; for analogies even when appropriate are little more than suggestive or at least corroborative of relations or conceptions which owe their main support to other and more sturdy evidence. Analogy under careful supervision may make a useful apprentice, but endless havoc results when the servant plays the part of the master.

No better illustrations could be desired of the effects of mental prepossession and the resulting distortion of evidence and of logical insight, than those afforded by Spiritualism and Christian Science. In both these movements the assimilation of a religious trend has been of inestimable importance to their dissemination. Surely it is not merely or mainly the evidences obtainable in the séance chamber, nor the irresistible accumulation of cures by argument and thought-healings, that account for the organized gatherings of Spiritualists and the costly temples and thriving congregations of Christ Scientist. It is the presentation of a practical doctrine of immortality and of the spiritual nature of disease in conjunction with an accepted religious system that is responsible for these vast results. The 'Key to the Scriptures' has immeasurably reinforced the 'Science and Health,' and brought believers to a new form of Christianity who never would have been converted to a new system of medicine presented on purely intellectual grounds. Rationality is doubtless a characteristic tendency of humanity, but logicality is an acquired possession and one by no means firmly established in the race at large. So long as we are reproved by the discipline of nature and that rather promptly, we tend to act in accordance with the established relations of things; and that is rationality. But the more remote connections between antecedent and consequent and the development of habits of thought which shall lead to reliable conclusions in complex situations; and again, the ability to distinguish between the plausible and the true, the firmness to support principle in the face of paradox and seeming non-conformity, to think clearly and consistently in the absence

The Modern Occult

of the practical reproof of nature — that is logicality. It is only as the result of a prolonged and conscientious training aided by an extensive experience and a knowledge of the historical experience of the race, that the inherent rational tendencies develop into established logical habits and principles of belief. For many this development remains stunted or arrested; and they continue as children of a larger growth, leaning much on others, rarely venturing abroad alone and wisely confining their excursions to familiar ground. When they unfortunately become possessed with the desire to travel, their lack of appreciation of the sights which their journeys bring before them gives to their reports the same degree of reliability and value as attaches to the much ridiculed comments of the philistine *nouveaux riches*.

For these sufficient reasons it is Utopian to look forward to the day when the occult shall have disappeared, and the lion and the lamb shall feed and grow strong on the same nourishment. Doubtless new forms and phases of the occult will arise to take the place of the old as their popularity declines; and the world will be the more interesting and more characteristically a human dwelling-place for containing all sorts and conditions of minds. None the less it is the plain duty and privilege of each generation to utilize every opportunity to dispel error and superstition, and to oppose the dissemination of irrational beliefs. It is particularly the obligation of the torch-bearers of science to illuminate the path of progress and to transmit the light to their successors with undiminished power and brilliancy; this flame must burn both as a beacon-light to guide the wayfarer along the highways of advance and as a warning against the will-of-the-wisps that shine seductively in the bye-ways. The safest and most efficient antidote to the spread of the pernicious tendencies inherent in the occult lies in the cultivation of a wholesome and whole-souled interest in the genuine and profitable problems of nature and of life, and in the cultivation with it of a steadfast adherence to common sense and to a true logical perspective of the significance and value of things. These qualities, fortunately for our forefathers, are not the prerogative of the modern; and, fortunately for posterity, are likely to remain characteristic of the scientific and antagonistic to the occult.

Joseph Jastrow

ISBN : 978-1532980367